Volume 61 of the
Yale Series of Younger Poets,
edited by Dudley Fitts
and published with aid from
the Mary Cady Tew Memorial Fund.

Dream Barker

and other poems

by Jean Valentine

Foreword by Dudley Fitts

New Haven and London:

Yale University Press, 1965

Grateful acknowledgment is made to
American Scholar, Atlantic Monthly, and Yale Review
for permission to include four poems
which originally appeared in these periodicals.

for my mother and father

Foreword

Three of Miss Valentine's poems struck me at first reading and remained to haunt me long after I had closed her manuscript. I do not mean that I found no others to praise, for the pages were bright with good things; and I do not intend, in this brief introduction, to demonstrate the triad, or explicate it, or attempt to suggest more for it than it will bear. The proper editorial gesture, I suppose, is general and choric: it is the poems, and the poems as a whole, that provide the central, engrossing action. A sponsor, however, especially when he has been as much moved as I have been, may be permitted a few curtailed *responsoria*.

'This way love's conversation, the body and mind of it': the text is Miss Valentine's and it controls her work. Her ideas, her images, her very modes of saying, spring from love in its various aspects: from love of persons and places revisited, from love in experience, in contemplation, in dream. The antagonist Anterôs, in whatever dismaying or calamitous shapes, is here as well; for the poems constitute a dialectic, a true conversation. The themes are ancient and common, the proper themes of lyric—youth, passion, loss, the human outrage, death. They are as old as poetry itself. What renews them here is a quirkily singular intelligence, a fusion of wit and tenderness, subserved by an unusual accuracy of pitch and rightness of tone. Insight and art work a transmutation.

'First Love,' for example, is an amusing and disconcerting version of ordinary experience. The first shock, I suppose, comes from its surface exuberance, the darting electrical interplay of epithet and image. All of us began in the sea, or so the scientists seem to tell us, and our forefathers deduced Aphroditê from the foam. Miss Valentine welcomes both the pedantry and the theophany and gives us back an erotic vision in sub-marine terms.

Superficially it is all amorous play, a dance of innocent and not-so-innocent grotesques:

> my love,
> My double, my Siamese heart, my whiskery,
> Fish-belly, glue-eyed prince—

but the surface is illusory. These aquarium shapes are disturbingly ambiguous: are they amusement or horror? Even the syntax, thanks to a deft handling of parallelism and lineation, reflects the ambivalence: the tug on the word 'whiskery,' for instance, which we take as a noun, though a queer one, until the following adjectives pull it into their construction. The uncertainty is pervasive, affecting even the identity of the apostrophized lover, and we become aware, beneath the surface thus disturbed, of a ritual of distressing self-encounter, of pride and shame in self, the enactment of something primal in us, a meeting

> Aping the man, liebchen! my angel, my own!
> How deep we met, how dark,
> How wet! before the world began.

Here is anxiety, if you like, the very upholstery of the clinical couch. But how it is transformed! The cascading of language, the nervous twining diversions of the verse line, the vivacity of comic insight, the tenderness, the extraordinary, almost tactile illusion of a voice speaking: here is poetry energizing the common theme, here is the making new.

The mode of 'First Love' is contemplative and declamatory. In 'A Bride's Hours' it is dramatic, the inner monologue. Each of the three panels of the triptych is autonomous, but each is affected by an impinging radiation from the others. It is a delight to watch Miss Valentine's mutations of trope and image from one monologue to another: 'Bachrach's rectangle' and the 'childish outline' pass from the first section to become the bowl, the mirror, the 'hollow circle closed by the ring' of the second, and these in turn are echoed in the enclosing hand, the glove, the lake, of the third. But it is the drama, the action, that says most here. The bride's sisters, her attendants, are attractively bored as they

> walk around touching things, or loll
> On the bed with last month's *New Yorkers*,—

but there is something oddly out of kilter, dehumanized, in their chatter. Their voices

> whir like cardboard birds
> On sticks: married, they flutter and wheel—

Cardboard, not real; controlled, moreover, by toy 'sticks', which a mercilessly accurate colon glosses as 'married'; but

> it is time to come in
> From thinking about the cake to eat the cake,

and what is ominous in expectation, the 'centaur dreams . . . of man and horse', will die away in the sleep of exhaustion. The numbed rimes of the last section, the iteration of 'hand', risk everything at the end, but the poet's daring is movingly successful. The drama is complete.

'To My Soul', my final instance, combines these modes. Unlike the poems I have been discussing, it is overtly a literary poem, a paraphrase—indeed, it is a paraphrase of a paraphrase. That is to say, once upon a time the Emperor Hadrian addressed a whimsical poem to his soul, and the lines beginning

> *Animula uagula blandula*
> *hospes comesque corporis*

have inspired all sorts of imitations, not the least of them being Alexander Pope's heroically mistaken

> Vital spark of heavenly flame!
> Quit, oh quit this mortal frame!

One of the finer imitations is by Pierre de Ronsard, dictated on his deathbed in 1585. Hadrian's diminutives were another poetic risk, of course, and Ronsard has been audacious, even to the point of playing with his own name:

> *Amelette Ronsardelette,*
> *mignonnelette doucelette,*
> *treschere hostesse de mon corps,*
> *tu descens là bas foiblelette,*
> *pasle, maigrelette, seulette,*
> *dans le froid Royaulme des mors.*

A delicate and perilous game, and a single false step would have plunged the whole thing into silliness. But there is no false step, nor is there any in Miss Valentine's version:

> Scattered milkweed, valentine,
> Moonlighting darling, leonine
> Host and guest—

Admittedly, she has the advantage (like Ronsard) of a name that can bear the dangerous weight of this playing. That is endearing —a bonus, we might say. It is only one invention out of many, however, and it is in the oddnesses, the tumbling quirks of allusion and special diction—'uncut, unribboned mistletoe', 'gemmy toad', 'Symplegadês of every road'—that the sweet tension is built up. The poem, then, is literary only on the sur- face. It is no more a translation of Ronsard's than Ronsard's was of Hadrian's, though for its total effect it depends upon both; and though her conclusion looks back rather to the Emperor:

> *nec ut soles dabis iocos*

than to the Frenchman:

> *Passant, j'ay dict: suy ta fortune;*
> *ne trouble mon repos, je dor . . .*

she has combined the magic of both poets in a new and memorable utterance of her own. The poem speaks for itself.

DUDLEY FITTS

Contents

First Love

How deep we met in the sea, my love,
My double, my Siamese heart, my whiskery,
Fish-belly, glue-eyed prince, my dearest black nudge,
How flat and reflective my eye reflecting you
Blue, gorgeous in the weaving grasses
I wound round for your crown, how I loved your touch
On my fair, speckled breast, or was it my own turning;
How nobly you spilled yourself across my trembling
Darlings: or was that the pull of the moon,
It was all so dark, and you were green in my eye,
Green above and green below, all dark,
And not a living soul in the parish
Saw you go, hélas!
Gone your feathery nuzzle, or was it mine,
Gone your serpentine
Smile wherein I saw my maidenhood smile,
Gone, gone all your brackish shine,
Your hidden curl, your abandoned kill,
Aping the man, liebchen! my angel, my own!
How deep we met, how dark,
How wet! before the world began.

For a Woman Dead at Thirty

No one ever talked like that before, like your
Last white rush in the still light of your
Last, bungled fever: no one will any more.

Now we breathe easier: Love,
Released from itself, blows words of love all over,
Now your hands are crossed down there.

We wanted your whole body behind glass,
And you left just half a foot-print,
Half-smiling.

All night, driving,
I wanted to know:
At the turn of light that somewhere
Must still be cock's crow

You smiled slantwise in the side mirror,
Six months dead: *here's Romance*:
You wanted to know.

You Never, you blazing
Negative, o you wavering light in water,
Water I stir up with a stick: wavering rot,

O my sister!
                    even if I'd known,
All I could have said was that I know.

Dream Barker
and other poems

Miles from Home

Grown, and miles from home, why do I shy
From every anonymous door-slam or dull eye?
The giant-step, the yawn
That streaked my dreams twenty years ago are gone;
The hero and nurse, the smashing Rubens hoof
And fist, the witch who rode my bedroom roof
And made my finger bleed, after all are man and wife
Whose mortal ribs I cracked to water my life,
Whose eyes I weighted keeping my late hours,
Loving my boys, chain-smoking in late, dead bars,
Watching the first light pickle Storrow Drive.
Why did I need that empty space to live?
The hand in the dark was my own, God knows whose cars.

The clay gods lean, and cast shadows under the stars,
Enjoying the blameless flowers on their Boston roof.
The watering-can's bland nozzle gleams like a hoof.

To Salter's Point

Frances Wadsworth Valentine
1880–1959

Here in Framingham, black, unlikely
Wheel spoking into mild Republican townships,
I have come to where the world drops off
Into an emptiness that cannot bear
Or lacks the center to compel
The barest sparrow feather's falling.
Maybe our mortal calling
Is, after all, to fall
Regarded by some most tender care:
But here, the air
Has grown too thin: the world drops off
That could imagine Heaven, or so much care.

Framingham is building. The savage ring
And shake of the drill turn up your morphined sleep.
I fall, still in earth's monstrous pull,
To kiss your hands, your planeless face.
Oh, you are right
Not to know your death-bed's place;
To wander in your drugs from Framingham
To Salter's Point, the long blond beaches where
You and your brothers peeled oranges and swam
While your parents looked on in daguerreotype.
Your iron bedstead there was white like this:
And in this grave, unspeakable night,
Beyond the pull of gravity or care,
You have no place: nor we:

You have taken the summer house, the hedge,
The brook, the dog, our air, our ground down with you,
And all the tall gray children can run
Away from home now and walk forever and ever
And come to nothing but this mouthful of earth,
All endings over.

Lines in Dejection

for my sister

Remember how we spread our hair on the sea,
Phosphorous fans, the moon's edge crumbling under
Moving pieces of sky? Ghostly weeds loitered
Like misty Thetis's hair, or some sea-monster's
Ancient whiskers, floating around our knees;
Moony children, we drifted, and no god or monster
Could have seemed foreign then to our globe of water.
Remember
Lying like still shells on the glass water?
The paper moon opened, a Japanese water flower
Drifting free of its shell in the bowl of the sky.

Who poured it out? In twenty years
The bay is still in its place, they are still there,
Walking slowly by the water.
Have they been here, all along? Have we?
Back, back, I strike out from the ancestral stare
And now the bowl's shadow composes what I see:
The weeds cradle me and draw me under, under.
But there they are, on the pitch-black ocean floor,
Hands out, hair floating: everywhere!
Holding us in their charred arms like water.

Sleep Drops Its Nets

Sleep drops its nets for monsters old as the Flood;
You are not you, no more than I am I;
If our dead fathers walk the wall at night
Our hands when we wake up are white on white
Betraying neither wounds nor blood;
The voice is mist that made us cry.

And then day sweeps the castle dry.

Déjà-vu

No, my father here, as You said,
When I asked him for bread
Didn't refuse me; but the bread was green;
And now You!
Now I'm dry and cold,
Chattering in the corner of the greenhouse,
Now You let me know it was always You,
That déjà-vu
Tilt of the sunlight on the floor,
That silence at the door!
I'd laugh, but I never, never loved You,
And here I am dead,
My Midas teeth on edge, green
Jade on jade.

Sunset at Wellfleet

A spit of sky, awash with Venetian gold
Hangs over the Congregational bell-tower, where
Last night the Northern Lights sifted their fire,
Shot through with the airless dark, romantic and cold.
The sun doesn't move, but suddenly is gone,
The cloudy tide goes out, and leaves a ring.
Easy to die: we knew it all along:
Knee-high to the dark as of old:
These words I tell you smoking in my eye:
The tree-frog is the tree-frog. The sky is the sky,
The rattling bay runs night and day *I, I, I,*
Over and over, turning on itself: there,
Where it curls on emptiness: there I sing.

Asleep over Lines from Willa Cather

Now I lay me desolate to sleep
Cold in the sound of the underground flood,
Brushed in half-sleep by the phantom plant
Pressed in the book by my bed
Blue-green leaves, large and coarse-toothed . . .
With big white blossoms like Easter lilies . . .
Latour recognized the noxious datura.
In its dead shade I lay me down to sleep.

The reins inside my head that hold my hope
When it leaps, in waking life, fall slack,
And, beyond the world of falling things,
With flesh like air, and an assumed agreement
Between my body and the way it takes,
I walk aimlessly by a green and perfect river.

The garden is here, as I knew it would be;
The garden imagined through oblique windows in paintings,
Earth's lost plantation, waiting for all, all,
All to be well: the fountain translates the sun.
I do not see but know God follows me,
And I follow, without fear of madness,
Paths and turnings that are both wild and formal,
Of all colors or none, tiger-lily and rock,
Pools dead with the weight of fallen leaves, and falls,
Follow after him I love, who waits in the garden.

Mercy, Pity, Fear and Shame
Spring in this garden, for it is earth's.
My body is not air, it casts a shadow.
At the next turning I come upon him I love
Waiting by the tree from my childhood that drops
White petals that hugely snow on the whitening ground.
He takes my arm and we walk a little way
Away from the tree towards the shining river
Running clear green through the garden.

The allegorists' arrow has struck me down.
I freeze in the noise of the flood.
When my love bends to speak, it is a language
I do not know: I answer and have no voice,
I am deaf, I am blind, I reach out to touch his face
And touch a spot of spittled clay, my eye,
Hiding the garden, the river, the tree.

Cambridge by Night

Down the aisles of this dark town
Pass faces and faces I have known
In the green, dog days, I forget their names,
Forget their faces.

Every public place in this city
Is a sideshow of souls sword-swallowing pity:
Father Dog-face barks without a sound,
The penny candles stare me down.

You were so close I could have touched the dead
Childhood in your face,
Left my mother's house a bride
With a light,
Night-light, dawn, to be by your side
All night,
But wanting pity, pity stood
Between us in your face.

Nothing troubles the dark: the last
Tiffany windows are out. Their ghosts
Might be my dutch uncles; pity
It's summer, they're out of the city.

To a Friend

I cannot give you much or ask you much.
Though I shore myself up until we meet,
The words we say are public as the street:
Your body is walled up against my touch.

Our ghosts bob and hug in the air where we meet,
My reason hinges on arcs you draw complete,
And yet you are walled up against my touch.

Your love for me is, in its way, complete,
Like alabaster apples angels eat,
But since it is in this world that we meet
I cannot give you much or ask you much.

You go your way, I mine, and when we meet,
Both half-distracted by the smells of the street,
Your body is walled up against my touch.

My body sings at your table, waits on the street
And you pass empty-handed, till when we meet
I have been so far, so deep, so cold, so much,
My hands, my eyes, my tongue are like bark to the touch.

Waiting

Ask, and let your words diminish your asking,
As your journal has diminished your days,
With the next day's vanity drying your blood,
The words you have lost in your notebooks.
Ask—do not be afraid. Praise Him for His silence.

What I love to ask is what I know,
Old thoughts that fit like a boot.
What I would hazard clings in my skull:
Pride intervenes, like an eyelid.

All sound slows down to a monstrous slow repetition,
Your times of reflection become a dark shop-window,
Your face up against your face.
You kneel, you see yourself see yourself kneel,
Revile your own looking down at your looking up;
Before the words form in the back of your head
You have said them over and answered, lives before.
O saints, more rollicking sunbeams, more birds about your heads!
Catherine, more Catherine-wheels!

Sic transit gloria mundi,
The quick flax, the swollen globe of water.
Sic transit John's coronation, mortal in celluloid.
Underground roots and wires burn under us.
John outlives the Journal's 4-color outsize portrait
Suitable for Framing, flapping, no color,
No love, in the rain on the side of the paper-shed.

Into Thy hands, O Lord, I commit my soul.
All Venice is sinking.

Let us dance on the head of a pin
And praise principalities!

Life is a joke and all things show it!
Let us praise the night sounds in Connecticut,
The Czechoslovak's parakeet,
Whistling *Idiot, Idiot!*

The moon's disk singes a bucketing cloud
Lit by the sun lit by a burning sword
Pointing us out of the Garden.

Turn your back on the dark reflecting glass
Fogged up with the breath of old words:

You will not be forgiven if you ignore
The pillar of slow insistent snow
Framing the angel at the door,
Who will not speak and will not go,

Numbering our hairs, our bright blue feathers.

Sasha and the Poet

Sasha: I dreamed you and he
Sat under a tree being interviewed
By some invisible personage. You were saying
'They sound strange because they were lonely,
The seventeenth century,
That's why the poets sound strange today:
In the hope of some strange answer.'
Then you sang '*hey nonny, nonny, no*' and cried,
And asked him to finish. '*Quoth the potato-bug,*'
He said, and stood up slowly.
'By Shakespeare.' And walked away.

The Second Dream

We all heard the alarm. The planes were out
And coming, from a friendly country. You, I thought,
Would know what to do. But you said,
'There is nothing to do. Last time
The bodies were like charred trees.'

We had so many minutes. The leaves
Over the street left the light silver as dimes.
The children hung around in slow motion, loud,
Liquid as butterflies, with nothing to do.

A Bride's Hours

for Arthur Platt

I. DAWN

I try to hold your face in my mind's million eyes
But nothing hangs together. My spirit lies
Around my will like an extra skin
I cannot fill or shake.
My eyes in Bachrach's rectangle look in.
I, who was once at the core of the world,
Whose childish outline held like a written word,
Am frozen in blur: my body, waiting, pours
Over its centaur dreams, and drowns, and wakes
To terror of man and horse.

2. THE BATH

My sisters walk around touching things, or loll
On the bed with last month's *New Yorker*s. My skin,
Beaded with bath-oil, gleams like a hot-house fake:
My body holds me like an empty bowl.
It is three, it is four, it is time to come in
From thinking about the cake to eat the cake.
My sisters' voices whir like cardboard birds
On sticks: married, they flutter and wheel to find
In this misted looking-glass their own lost words,
In the exhaled smoke.
                           There isn't a sound,
Even the shadows compose like waiting wings.
I am the hollow circle closed by the ring.

3. NIGHT

I am thrown open like a child's damp hand
In sleep. You turn your back in sleep, unmanned.
How can I be so light, at the core of things?
My way was long and crooked to your hand!
What could your jewelled glove command
But flight of my stone wings?
Our honeymoon lake, ignoring the lit-up land,
Shows blank Orion where to dip his hand.

Afterbirth

I loiter in the eye of the Slough,
Every joint aching for sleep;
The sky, inhumanly deep,
Sarcastically casts back the Slough.

Did my child take breath to cry
At the slick hand that hooked her out,
Or cry to breathe? or did she lie
Still in her private dark, curled taut

Under her sleep's hobgoblin shout?
Anaesthesia blew me out:
I gardened shadows in my lost crib
While they took her from me like a rib.

Swaddled and barred, she curls in sleep
At the dry edge of mortality.
If the sky's side proves too steep
Who will take up the little old lady,

Who will call her by her name
When she's a crumble of bones?
What logos lights the filament of time,
Carbon arc fusing birth-stone to head-stone?

The mud pulls harder: the stepping stones
Shake in front of my swimming eyes.
There dear, there dear, here's a pill:
Sleep, sleep, all will be well:
Lull-lullaby.

Sarah's Christening Day

Our Lord, today is Sarah's christening day.
I wouldn't build the child a house of straw,
Teach her to wait and welcome the holy face
With candles of prayer, or pray, if the wager were all.
But I have never seen or loved the holy face.
I don't believe the half of what I pray.

This world is straw: straw mother, father, friend,
Per omnia saecula saeculorum, amen.
But Lord! it shines, it shines, like light, today.

Tired of London

When you came to town,
Warm bubbling rains came, the teething leaves,
Steaming spring earth, and the tough, small-footed birds;

Reckless colors sifted the closed, dense sky
As we went hand in hand through our larky maze
In the cultivated stubble of Hampstead Heath:

Monkshood, Foxglove, Canterbury Bells
Composed themselves to drink the bovril air
Thinned by the watery sun.

You, with no sense of giving,
Brought all the dangers I no longer dared;
Netted the wind that roared through my rented bed,

And, poised like Eros over Picadilly,
Were always there.
I cannot find the words to leave you with.

This way love's conversation, the body and mind of it, goes
On after love: we shall come to call this love,
And this roar in our ears which before very long
We become, we shall call our song.

Cambridge
April 27, 1957

Your letter made me see myself grown old
With only the past's poor wing-dust shadows to hold,
Dressed in violet hand-me-downs, half-asleep, only half,
Queer as nines in the violet dust of my mind,
Leaning in some sloping attic, like this one where I write
You all night,
The wet, metaphorical Cambridge wind
Sorry on the skylight.
                    The New England landscape goes
Like money: but here on Agassiz Walk we save
Everything we have
Under Great-Aunt Georgie's georgian bed;
A knot garden roots through Great-Aunt Georgie's toes
Three floors below: when summer comes, God knows
We'll dry the herbs Aunt Georgie grows:
Who knows, who knows
What goes on in her head.

I read Thoreau myself, I listen for Thoreau
Up here; wonder if there's a burial mound
Anywhere for Henry: PAX, ÆTAT.
45. Quiet Desperation. REQUIESCAT,

Ducky: one of these nice days
My niece, the one with one glass eye,
Is driving me out to Walden Pond:
Cross my heart, I hope to die.

New York
April 27, 1962

When we get old, they say, we'll remember
Things that had sunk below the mind's waking reach
In our distracted years; someday, knees blanketed, I will reach out
To touch your face, your brown hair.

Remember now thy Creator in the days of thy youth.
I rest, tending children, in hollow, light rooms,
Sleep in their milky fingers, after years
Howling up on the tiles while my goblins threw their shoes.
The child I carry lies alone:
Which hag did we not invite to its conception?
I cat-nap, remembering the tiles.

And you?
Steps on the sidewalk outside my barred New York windows
Land on the cracks, let out the bears,
Loose them on the child who is not there;
Footsteps that gleam in their echo of SS men's heels
Off-stage in my first movies: approaching the door.
We huddle inside and wake to remember it's Peace.
Peace. But you are not here, nor are you dead.

No-one forgot my birthday. Twenty-eight.
How shall we celebrate?
Fetch my blanket, dearest, there's something in the air,
Dark, quick, quicksilver, dark eyes, brown hair,
Bringing all the presents: someone is coming late:
The babies cry, the bell rings in thin air.

September 1963

We've been at home four years, in a kind of peace,
A kind of kingdom: brushing our yellow hair
At the tower's small window,
Playing hop-scotch on the grass.

With twenty other Gullivers
I hover at the door,
Watch you shy through this riddle of primary colors,
The howling razzle-dazzle of your peers.

Tears, stay with me, stay with me, tears.
Dearest, go: this is what
School is, what the world is.
Have I sewed my hands to yours?

Five minutes later in the eye of God
You and Kate and Jeremy are dancing.

Glad, derelict, I find a park bench, read
Birmingham. Birmingham. Birmingham.
White tears on a white ground,
White world going on, white hand in hand,
World without end.

Riverside

Now, with March forcing our brittle spines like first childbirth,
Scattering our notes, making the house cold inside,
Riverside Park turns up its vestiges of God
Where bare-faced boys in their sweat-suits lope through the last light
Alongside long-haired girls, half-tree,
And every dog is a brother, or half-brother,
And the cold-war babies span their tender fists,
198?, to net the sun
Spun gold in these thousand pigeon brown windows
Then OUT in a mushroom of neon over Hoboken:
And I, like you, am I, in the eyes of the angels.

Winter was the time for the kind of death we enjoyed:
Then the crust of the earth was something arbitrary;
Branches roots, the sky a vein of tin,
Leaves rose, smoke fell, all the old ladies
Waiting on the benches grew beards waiting.
We talked on the phone, napped, grew white and dry
And leapt at misunderstanding, forcing the news
Every day, the news of the end of love
From the earth's four corners: then left home in the dark,
Dropping pebbles behind us, came
Into the cold: tears from the cold
Stood in our eyes like tears.

Now, with March,
The woods begin to move, and I
Hold your body in my mind, and see
In each man here a mooning orphan boy,
In every long-haired girl a bearded lady,
In every dog the green part of my mind.
That couple stops: tenderly
He carves their initials in her bright green bark.
She takes a child, the moon climbs one slow step
And stands alone; and I
Keep in and chip in my sleep at winter's bone.

For Teed

April 6th: the country thaws and drips,
The worm turns under the town,
Under the world: the freed earth gapes
In wily Ulysses' lips,
The dust of his wrist rests
In caves that were Penelope's breasts,
Even the dog is gone
White-eyed to Acheron:
No Elizabeth, no Jack
Has come back.
Here lies Teed.
Surviving her are

God, can you hear her
Sing? how earth is freed
Of Teed's winter,
Morphine, flowers
Curled on the radiator,
Freed of her visiting hours,
The night sounds of St. Luke's,
Of her fortune-cookie body, freed
Of the whole table reading *cancer*:
The needle trembles, breaks!
Her face swells: can you hear?
Freed of her! of her!

My Grandmother's Watch

Your first child was my father,
Old *muti* of Buffalo, little old child heiress,
My black-eyed baby, chain-smoking gold-
Tipped English Ovals in Heaven: your brassy
Churchillian French reduced us all to *mots*,
Even from the hardly troubled, lavendered sheets of your deathbed.

I wear your coin-thin red gold watch now, Momma,
Its face benign as the Archduke's, and think of your hours,
And what has gone between us, what is ours.
Tonight, for instance: my tongue is thick with longing:
When the children's visit was over, the cake cleared away,
What possessed your mahogany beasts to stay?

On the night of my eighteenth birthday
You made me a toast, saying I
Was not only good at school, but musical!
Pink-cheeked, black-hearted, shy,
I couldn't even look you in the eye:
They cleared the cake away.

The insanely steady minute-hand sweeps round,
The hours go by. Somebody said
His Viennese grandfather
Sold him his watch on his deathbed.
Did you too?

What can I do?

O Momma, what can I
Do with this gold and crystal that goes by?

The Beast with Two Backs

for James

Excursion: a night, two days
Away from home and neighborhood,
Double-locked doors, mirror-
Backed peep-holes: the neighbors.

How big they've grown, the children!
Make them walk! It's not good,
A woman, the insides! Daughters,
You'll always have them; five sons,
One's in Teaneck. Make her walk!
You'll break your mother's back!

The boat: by Christ, an excursion.
Every man has seven wives, each wife
Has seven children, each child has seven guns.
The ladies change, they do change, in the Ladies'
Room: they wink, they shrug, they look over their backs
At their colorful tails. I look at my toes
In the stall where the toilet roils with the white Atlantic.

Over the *Times* we talk about Ho,
Allen Dulles, Malcolm X: take up our Signet Classics.
Someone across the way from us is reading *The Guermantes' Way*,
Who smiles. It is a long trip to our island,
Seven years already,
Longer than anyone ever would have thought.
We buy beer; I'd like
A colorful tail like that.

On our island we walk, eat, lie,
Drink, walk, analyze, analyze.
This moon we do not like we'll like
Remembering, and know it.
Do we trust ourselves more this morning?
Today we can stay in bed all day. Ah, love,

The soap, Irina! You have no soap! The sheets,
Irina, in Six! Knock knock.

Knock. We give it up, we are married
Seven years, we can smile with the backs of our heads:
The two-backed beast is wild,
We let him go.
                He said. She said.
He said.
      We turn our backs
For home.
         On the wall it said "For Fire:
Continuous ringing of bell and call of FIRE."

The Little Flower

I thank God, I have never taken to drinking, as many I know
       have, I have never done that and my children should be
       thankful but they are not, I have not been that kind,
I say my prayers every night,
Lots of them do and with less reason, I did once but put it from
       me, and with all the shocks I have had to bear, such shocks
       in those terrible years, you do not know, my father, my
       father was a mean man,
Given to giving nicknames,
He called me Susan B. Anthony because I was so strong I guess,
       I have never given way as others would have done, he
       called your aunt *Bunny* because when her first two teeth
       came in he said *she looks just like a bunny*, she did look just
       like a bunny, *we will call her Bunny* and so she is to this day
       I am eighty-three she must be eighty, strange she was al-
       ways jealous of my looks Bun was, I was tall and slim
And very beautiful they all said so,
And she thought I had all the looks always was a jealous kind of
       person but you know she was very lovely too, I was jeal-
       ous of her too, isn't that funny I always thought Bun had
       such nice feet and I always thought my feet were ugly
       isn't that funny, the things you will get into your head,
       feet
It hasn't all been roses,
My mother was a Ross a Ross from Scotland, they were a noble
       clan, your mother sent me a postcard once of the Ross
       castle, I have it somewhere in these suitcases, it's in the
       north
Oh I must set my things in order
I must have help to set my things in order, so many papers, no

one will come and soon I will be gone and then who will,
No now we will talk it is so good, to have someone to talk
to, is that chair all right for you not in a draft, this room
has a terrible draft you have beautiful eyes,
A little like mine oh when I was younger
You have always been a good child and you know you get funny
all alone in a room I hope I have never complained but
you get and at my age, no one understands what it is like
to be old, does my mind wander, that is what I
I forget things
Words do not come to my mind, my mother was a Ross from
Scotland, they were a noble clan, she used to tell such
wonderful stories and sing us the old songs she would go
on with those stories and songs the children loved her, she
came and visited us often and stayed weeks and weeks, she
was always there if I were sick, I hope she always knew she
had a home with us and I was sick so much with the cli-
mate what it was and the miscarriages and the babies, and
she always came to be a comfort to me, but then she died,
What it is like
He had died long before that, there is a place for Bun and a place
for me with them in the plot in Minneapolis, I don't care
about cremation it seems the cleanest thing you don't
mind talking about these things do you, neither do I some
people do but I don't mind talking about these things at
all, look at my teeth, if I do not get to the dentist, but I
cannot even get dressed, just to get dressed but I get so
dizzy, when I stand I am so afraid of falling again, will you
look at my teeth, I try not to smile so as to show them, I
always had beautiful teeth

It seems the cleanest thing

Bunny has written me a long letter about it, she's going to be
cremated, Henry was too, you pack a bag with the clothes
you want to go in and if you go in winter like her Henry
did, and a godsend, they wait till Spring to put you in the
ground, Henry's there, no I don't mind about cremation as
long as they make sure I'm good and dead first, ha, ha,

Look at my teeth

The children loved her, she would tell them those stories over and
over, no I don't remember any of them, not one, and the
children don't any more, I asked Louise and she said, No
Mother, I like to tell you these things because soon I will
be gone and then no one will remember all this

My father

There do you hear her, there she goes, eight or ten hours a day
some days, they say she is an opera singer, it goes right
through my spine, we would always come to New York
here for the opera season, we always took the same suite
at the Plaza Hotel, the manager was a very fine gentleman,
he always said to me, Mrs. Haran, your children are the
best behaved children who have ever visited us here at the
Plaza Hotel, and they were, so quiet

They all said so

Your grandfather used to love the operas and then we always
had season tickets for the Chicago Symphony, I would
take the children every Friday afternoon, do you hear her,
I have sent a note to the desk but they say there is nothing
they can do, I must take another room, on another floor,
another hotel

Just to get dressed

Your mother always had a gift for music, she had lessons from
the age of five with the best piano teacher in the city, but
no when she married him she let it go, I told her, you will
be sorry Louise, if you have music you will always have
that whatever comes, like books, my children all loved
books if you give children the love of books they will always have that whatever comes, will you listen to that
woman, I have told them at least let her be still Sundays,
at least let me have peace Sundays but you know they are
all Jewish people in this hotel
Not that I
Not that I have anything against Jewish people if you like them
I hope I am not so narrow, it is all knishes, what are they,
and lox and the good Lord knows what on the menu, I
cannot eat it, Ramón my waiter says ¡Ah Mrs. Haran
you did not eat! they all loved reading, if I could only read
but it hurts my eyes so
Even the Tribune
With everything else I had to bear there were always books, I
used to read a book a day, oh yes and magazines, Edward
used to tease me for taking the Post but I have always said
there are lots of fine articles in the Post I still take it but now
I can hardly read the Tribune, Dr. Giroux wants me to
see an ophthalmologist
Just to get dressed
Edward your uncle Edward was a great reader, he was always
reading, he always said he loved to read with me there in
the room, we always read together like that when he was
little, those were bad years, that was when it was just beginning, he was reading to himself at three years, his

37

teachers always told me, Eddie has a wonderful mind, they called him Eddie, I was always with him when he was little, that was when your grandfather began to take too much, then I was so ill and Edward would always come in and sit by me, I was in bed so much, months at a time, Edward would say Mother shall I sit with you a while, he was always considerate that way most children are not you know, Edward was

To be a comfort

They were seven brothers the children's uncle Jack was first, the monsignor, then your grandfather, and the others were all born over here, well they scattered around the middle west, mostly farming and such, your grandfather was the only one of them who ever made his way, and Jack, one went to California I think, oh the Lord knows where they all are now living or dead, they all blamed me

Listen to her

We had an audience with the Pope did I ever tell you that I like to tell you these things, Pope Pius X, he was a very charming man, charming, a gentleman I shall never forget it, a private audience, no he spoke English, your uncle Jack was at the American College, he arranged it all, no I went to the Church long before I ever met your grandfather I was still at home well it seemed to draw me in I don't know why, my father said it was just like me, *The Little Flower* he called me

A religious man, they were all religious men

I have always held that your church doesn't matter as long as you live right you must give the children some faith to stand by them when their troubles come, it doesn't matter what

38

church I hope I am not so narrow, but it breaks my heart
to see Billy and her raising those children without anything, he always went to the best Catholic schools, I gave
him that, and how can he stand by and watch her raise
those children with nothing, and how can she let him get
so heavy

It's the drinking

I'm sorry, I hope I've always been good to her the same as I am
with all of you yet she never brings them, they are my
grandchildren and I never see them, they do not know
me, they lose that you know, they will never have those
memories, it is nice to have a sense of family

They all blamed me

We went down, Jack had a summer place at that castle Gandolfo
you know, very nice, outside Rome, it was hot, I remember I was faint do you hear her ah-ah-ah-ah, no no coffee
for me I can't take it, my lower intestine, well, and then
I get so terribly dizzy, Dr. Giroux has given me pills for
it but I don't like to take them, just some ice water is all,
there in that green bottle, Tipperary was where they came
from but they were originally Normans

Normans who came over from France

Jack was good to us at first, for a while, at the beginning he would
take his dinner with us every night, so as to keep the idea
of a family for the children, he cared a lot for that, priests
do they don't know, that was when it was beginning with
your grandfather, the stocks dropping and his partner
and all and the never coming home

The children never knew

I spared them that, and the miscarriages, it was not so easy in

39

those days to have a baby, you girls today, and my back was never strong to carry them, six months in bed before Billy, and then the brothers tried to get me to have him back, they all blamed me

Normans

I was never off a penny in my books when I was spending thousands of dollars managing Astor Street and now I'm always so confused that is what terrifies me, my checkbook is in such a state and no one, I ask Billy but he never comes, I guess she won't let him away, I don't think much of a person like that, I like to keep two thousand dollars margin in case I have to go to the hospital or so when I go it will, but it's under that now I don't know how much and I make mistakes in my arithmetic, and then these medicines, forty dollars, fifty dollars, I feel awful, the children do not understand or they would not be so

What it is like

None of you, but you are a good child, I always had a special place in my heart even when you were little, of course I loved you all, and I worry so about you, when you get old you worry a lot, there's some nice cake in there on the shelf chocolate the kind you like, I got it in last week expecting you, oh I know how much you have to do at home, I hope you're through having children now, two is a nice family plenty these days, you know just a phone call would mean a lot when you have a minute

The children do not know

I hate to call you I know how busy you are, I hope I haven't asked much of my family, I know you're all caught up in your own life the family and all, you looked tired, I

40

loved my children I hope I loved my children

None of you

I hope I was good to him, everything a wife should be, he was
proud of me, all my clothes were made specially for me,
and I was never off a penny in my books and they all loved
to come to Astor Street, I remember Mr. Fairbank a mil-
lionaire there, he used to always come and he could have
had anything in the world, he loved to come to us, he
said, Nelly I feel at home here, a charming man, a very
old family, no airs, no I never turned him away while he
was well, I was everything a wife should be, it wasn't
easy but men are that way and I hope I never let him know
while he was well

Anything in the world

He used to say, Nelly, you make me feel very grateful, and he
tried to be very considerate that way while he was well,
not all men do, you know, he did try

Music whatever comes

What could I do, it was such a shock, the money, and then him
never coming home and the drinking, I had the children
to think of, they never knew, Jack tried to help him, first
talking himself then the doctors, but nothing helped, he
got worse, worse, he had had so much, risen from nothing
himself, and he became deluded after the drop, losing
more and more, he was on the telephone talking business
as if he were still what he had been, then I had to call back,
I was so ashamed, and explain he was not well, everyone
was very kind, I couldn't go out of the house

I had the children to think of

I kept everything just as it had been for them, Dr. Lapham their

doctor, he was a world-famous pediatrician, he died of
pneumonia in Boston, he had called on me the day before
he went just to see how we were getting along, he said,
Mrs. Haran try to do for the children just as you would
have done, and I did, Billy went to Canterbury and Har-
vard, Louise had a beautiful debut, I always had all her
clothes made specially for her and there wasn't a better
dressed girl her year, or a prettier, it wasn't as if we had a
lot

Dr. Lapham

But I always remembered what Dr. Lapham had said, many
women would not have done it that way for their children, I should have thought of my own old age

Dr. Lapham

They all blamed me when he was put in the mental home, it was
the best state institution in the middle west, I had the children to think of, they said there was money enough for
private care but I knew what there was and I knew he
couldn't be helped, we had spoken to the best doctors in
Chicago, do you know what the private places cost, and
he lived, he lived for years and years, he only died three
years ago, there wasn't that kind of money for him, look
how I've had to manage all these years, and I had to do for
the children it would all have gone, what would I have
done, no he hadn't lost much yet but he would have if
he'd gone on, I had to save what I could

I knew

They kept trying to get him away, one Christmas they got him
out, a trick, and brought him down to Minneapolis, it was
Christmas night, so cold, and we had to take him back, he

was not responsible then for what he said, he was ill the
doctors could not do anything for him, the money was
gone, all but what I had managed to keep away, I had the
children to think of, and myself

He was not responsible then

Then later Billy and your mother brought him east to another
state home, New York State, up here, they said it was a
better place, no they never visited him, he did not know
them anymore they said, that was when they were grown
of course when they were young they never knew

They all blamed me

Dr. Lapham did not blame me, I asked him, in the worst of it, I
had no one to turn to and I asked him and he said, it is very
hard Mrs. Haran, he understood and Edward understood
he was older than the others and I used to talk to him I
had no one, oh of course I didn't tell him the truth, but
he was with me and that was a comfort, Bun came but she
did not understand ever, she always thought he could be
helped by the doctors, she never understood

They all blamed me

We didn't see her for a long while and then we didn't talk about
it any more, but I knew she blamed me, she used to say, he
loves you Nelly, she never understood he had never loved
me never, only the house and the clothes and that

Edward understood

He was always with me if it hadn't been for Edward there were
times I would have commit suicide, I know it's a terrible
thing to say, but those were terrible years, but for Edward
who always understood, and he was always there, later I
wanted him to go out and get a place of his own, make

his life away from all my troubles, but he always said No
    Mother and he always stayed until he died four years ago,
    the night he died his car went over a bridge

It was the eye drops

He'd been reading Stendahl On Love, he was always a great
    reader, when he died the doctor came in the middle of the
    night and gave me an injection, she was so kind to me that
    country doctor, she understood

Edward understood

It is a terrible thing to lose a child, no matter how old they are
    they are always your children and you always worry, I
    gave them everything, and then he died, and the other
    two never come, what have I done, your mother came
    when he died to be with me, she blamed me, I know she
    blamed me

Never only the house

She did not know how it was with Edward, the drinking and the
    trouble, I never told anyone, he needed me, thank God
    I had the money to help him out of his trouble, it was
    always the same, I was always there

Died, died

I should have thought more of myself, other women would have
    saved for themselves, learn from your grandmother

Christmas night

What it is like to be old, and alone, and sick, and I worry so about
    money, not about leaving a lot behind, I have done enough
    I hope, but I don't know how long I'll last, which will go
    first, ha, ha, the money or me

Always the same

Every night when I lie down I think they'll find me in the morn-

ing, I always have the bag ready, that blue one dear you
should know, every night I wash my feet before I get into
bed, they never think what it is like,
The children loved her,
Thousands of dollars, I loved my children, I hope I loved my
children, what have I done that they are strangers to me,
sometimes at night when I can't sleep
Whatever comes
I never sleep till three or four in the morning or five and then at
eight or nine she starts up with her scales sometimes I think
I must have said something or done something to hurt
them, something I do not know, do you know? then I
pray
Deliver her soul, O Lord
And that has been a comfort to me these last years, though what
the Lord has done for me I don't know, I hope I've always
lived right, and surely the Lord should not refuse His
creatures
And let my cry come unto Thee
Most children are not you know, Edward was, they all blamed
me, always the same, gone, and then no one, look at my
teeth, I am afraid to die, you are young but you know
you get afraid
I knew
It's good to talk like this to someone, and then I like to tell you
these things, never, only the house, died, died, died, soon
I will be gone and then no one will remember, there do
you hear her, none of you.

Sex

All the years waiting, the whole, barren, young
Life long. The gummy yearning
All night long for the far white oval
Moving on the ceiling;
The hand on the head, the hand in hand;
The gummy pages of dirty books by flashlight,
Blank as those damaged classical groins;

Diffusion of leaves on the night sky,
The queer, sublunar walks.
And the words: the lily, the flame, the truelove knot,
Forget-me-not; coming, going,
Having, taking, lying with,
Knowing, dying;
The old king's polar sword,
The wine glass shattered on the stone floor.

And the thing itself not the thing itself,
But a metaphor.

Adam and Eve: Poem on Folded Paper

We dream of saving what
cannot
Can't touch through this glass
pane
Pain that cuts the green world
down
Down, derry down with my true
love
Loving the one human voice we
heard
Heard myself answer in a
dream
Dream now, Adam, and wake to find no
world
The world's a dance of spiders against this
pane
And pain is their condition.

Dream Barker

We met for supper in your flat-bottomed boat.
I got there first: in a white dress: I remember
Wondering if you'd come. Then you shot over the bank,
A Virgilian Nigger Jim, and poled us off
To a little sea-food barker's cave you knew.

What'll you have? you said. Eels hung down,
Bamboozled claws hung up from the crackling weeds.
The light was all behind us. To one side
In a dish of ice was a shell shaped like a sand-dollar
But worked with Byzantine blue and gold. *What's that?*

Well, I've never seen it before, you said,
And I don't know how it tastes.
Oh well, said I, *if it's bad,*
I'm not too hungry, are you? We'd have the shell . . .
I know just how you feel, you said

And asked for it; we held out our hands.
Six Dollars! barked the barker, *For This Beauty!*
We fell down laughing in your flat-bottomed boat,

And then I woke up: in a white dress:
Dry as a bone on dry land, Jim,
Bone dry, old, in a dry land, Jim, my Jim.

To My Soul

after Hadrian and Ronsard

for Michael

Scattered milkweed, valentine,
Moonlighting darling, leonine
Host and guest of my château,

Tender, yawning concubine,
Vine of my summer in decline,
Uncut, unribboned mistletoe,

Monstrous footprint in the snow,
Hypnotizing, gemmy toad,
My generations' cameo,

Symplegadês of every road,
Closet bones, unflowered sod,
Laugh, my little nuncio!